HOW TO ROCK YOUR BUDGET

Tips to Help Couples Create and Stay On Track with Their Budget

by Roseann Baisley

Copyright © 2016 by Roseann Baisley

All rights reserved. This book or any portion thereof may not be reproduced or used in any manner whatsoever without the express written permission of the publisher except for the use of brief quotations in a book review.

First Printing, 2016

ISBN-13: 978-1539494676
ISBN-10: 1539494675

DEDICATION

This book is dedicated to my parents who set an amazing example not only with their money habits but with their parenting style.

HOW TO ROCK YOUR BUDGET

You probably have been told that having debt is okay and that it's normal to pay on loans and credit cards all your life. Everyone does it. Society is convincing us that we deserve the latest electronics and brand new cars. Every day, businesses accept our credit cards and signatures on loans with open arms.

I am not okay with everyone else deciding my financial future and if you're reading this I'm thinking you are not okay with it either. It's time to take control of your own financial future!

Will you be less of a person or missing out on something great without those extra payments hanging around? Absolutely not! What you will have is a new found freedom with your money and a weight lifted off of you.

Let me tell you it's amazing! My husband and I experienced the frustration of having large debt weighing down on us. We didn't know where our money was going. We were tired of watching our money disappear and scared that some emergency would happen and we wouldn't be able to cover it. We were so busy worrying about today that we didn't even think about the future and if we would have any money left to retire someday. We were sick of this feeling and the strain it put on our marriage.

Enough was enough. We decided to shake things up by taking control of our financial future. Wow! It has been amazing on so many levels. We have paid off large amounts of debt and no longer use credit to buy the things we need or want. We are no longer letting anyone else decide what we do with our money. This has made a positive impact on our marriage and the level of our communication is amazing! Would you like to feel that way as well?

It's time for you to be proactive vs. reactive with your money. How are you going to start being proactive? Simple. Start doing a monthly budget!

You might think that doesn't sound very simple. It's a pain in the butt and it will limit what we can spend. Let me clear something up for you. A budget is not meant to keep you from doing things you want. It's the opposite. A budget can get you on track, so you can do what you want with your money and avoid ugly debt that creeps into your life. It's YOU taking control of your financial future!

READY TO START BUDGETING

The first time we did a budget it was a mess. Lots of guessing. Now that we have it figured out (believe me, it's still not perfect) I want to simplify the process for you. The tips and tricks I'm providing will help you rock your budget. It's time to drop the dozens of excuses why you can't do this.

I have included a budget sheet in this book for you to get started. If you prefer, you can create your own personalized budget in Excel or grab a piece of paper and pencil. There are some great options online like mint.com or everydollar.com. We started our budget on a spreadsheet and now use the online option. Both options are great but you need to decide what works best for you. Trial and error!

When we first started budgeting, it was overwhelming and we didn't know exactly what we were doing. We've have learned a lot since we started the process. This information I compiled is to help guide you through the process of creating your own rock star budget. Every household has different line items on their budget so don't get frazzled if you don't see something listed that you spend money on every month. Budgets need to be tailored to your needs. Are you ready? Let's get started!

BASIC BUDGET SHEET

EXPENSES FOR MONTH:		
Home:	*Budgeted*	*Spent*
Mortgage/Rent:		
Real Estate Taxes:		
Insurance:		
Repairs:		
Electricity:		
Gas:		
Water:		
Trash:		
Other:		
TOTAL:		
Transportation:		
Gas & Oil:		
Repairs:		
Licsense/Taxes:		
Car Replacement:		
Other:		
TOTAL:		
Lifestyle:		
Clothing:		
Cable/Sattelite:		
Internet:		
Phone:		
Home Products:		
Pet Supplies:		
Entertainment:		
Hair/Beauty:		
Donations/Giving:		
Other:		
TOTAL:		
Health:		
Gym Membership:		
Medications:		
Doctor Bills:		
Dentist:		
Optometrist:		
Other:		
TOTAL:		
Food:		
Groceries:		
Restaurants:		
Other:		
TOTAL:		

Loans/Debt:	Budget	Spent
Credit Card 1:		
Credit Card 2:		
Loan 1:		
Loan 2:		
Other:		

Income for month:	*Budgeted*	*Received*
Paycheck 1:		
Paycheck 2:		
Other:		
TOTAL:		
Savings:		
Emergency Fund:		
Retirement Fund:		
Other:		
TOTAL:		

TOTAL EXPENSES:		
TOTAL INCOME:		

Goals:	Projected Date	Actual Date
Pay off date (debt 1)		
Pay off date (debt 2)		
Pay off date (debt 3)		
Emergency Fund (3-6 mos)		
Other:		

Rock your budget!

STEPS TO A SUCCESSFUL BUDGET

1:     Enter the month on the top line. This simple step helps you avoid the confusion of which month you are viewing and so you add the correct income/expense for that month. Plan ahead and start working on your budget a couple weeks or month prior so it's ready to go. I also suggest that you look ahead a few months so you can plan for those upcoming expenses (holidays, quarterly payments, etc.).

2:     Put your projected income in the right column under budget. If you have irregular income do your best to average what you make each month. It won't be exact but at least you have a number to work with for your budget. In this case, I suggest listing the minimum income in your budget. It allows you some wiggle room in your budget if you bring in above that dollar amount. If you get paid the last couple days of the month, that income should still be included in that month's budget.

3.   Start gathering up your expenses. Pull out bank and credit card statements, monthly memberships, utilities and receipts. In the back of the book I include a debt worksheet to guide you in listing out your loans, credit card bills, etc.

This task can feel very overwhelming but I promise you it will get easier once you get a budget rolling. It took us about 3 months of budgeting before we felt like we had a handle on our expenses. Consider saving all receipts during the first couple months as you try to get your budget perfected. Put your bills in categories. Example: All clothing purchases in one category and all restaurant and coffee stops in a category together. This allows you to see how much you are spending in each category.

4. In step 2, you projected your income for the month. Now that is the amount of money you have to work within your budget. Start allocating those dollars under expenses and savings. You are probably freaking out right about now. When you first start budgeting you will probably run short with your income vs. expenses. BREATHE!

Let's go back and look at areas that you can make some cuts in your spending. You probably have a set amount you need for utilities, mortgage and car payment so you might not be able to adjust them. To find some extra dollars take a look at the Lifestyle and Food categories. Could you cut some of your expenses there? At first glance you might think there is no way you can cut any further but this is where you separate out your NEEDS/WANTS. Below I will talk about this more in detail. Also, later in this book, I include some awesome ways to free up extra money in your budget. If you are still struggling, you may need to find a way to increase your income.

5.	When you are preparing your budget, it's important to ask yourself what is a NEED vs. WANT. A good way to do this is by writing down the items in your budget that are a need and items that are a want. Examples would include, electricity, heat, water, rent or mortgage as needs. These are all things that you need to maintain the basic necessities of life. Wants are things that we enjoy or "feel" we need to have in our life. Examples would include cable, vacations, dining out, a housekeeper and manicures. These items can make your life easier or bring you joy so it's hard to look at them as wants but that is what category they fall under.

When your budget is tight and you are trying to pay off debt or build a savings, the "wants" category is the best area to dig for extra dollars. Does it mean you can't ever enjoy your wants? Absolutely not! Once you get comfortable with your budget and set goals with your money you are in the driver's seat. YOU (with your spouse) determine what your money does and how to allocate it.

6.	The goals are meant for you to push yourself to pay off debt. If you don't have any debt that is great! Then consider changing your goals towards saving or investing. If you do have debt, why not pay it off and get it out of your life. It's not a very good friend and it's costing you a lot of your hard earned money.

I suggest setting a target date to have it paid off. List it in your budget so you see it written down. Take it further by adding a visual chart and put it on your fridge. If you set a goal to pay off your $10,000 loan in 10 months, make a colorful chart that you mark every $1000 you have paid towards it. How excited will you be each time you mark off a $1000 dollars? Now imagine the excitement when you mark off the last $1000! You will be zooming to the moon! Visuals are a great way to follow through and succeed with your goals.

Remember: Any extra dollars you can put towards debt will make it go away faster. Think of all the awesome things you can do with the extra money if you don't have to send it to creditors each month (don't forget all the ugly interest you are paying too).

7. Do you have an emergency fund? What if your car breaks down and you don't have any money saved up to fix it? Or what if you are laid off from your job. How will you pay the bills? What are you feeling? Stressed, scared, defeated? Emergencies happen! Plan to save now so you can feel in control when they do.

There is a line item in the budget for an emergency fund. Experts suggest 3-6 months of your income should be in your emergency fund. If you are paying off debt, start with a smaller emergency fund (approx. $1,000-$2,000) so you can aggressively pay off your loans/credit cards that are holding you down. Once you have the debt paid, start putting more in your emergency fund.

Feeling overwhelmed with all of this? Take a deep breath and talk with your spouse about how you are feeling? Review WHY you are doing this. How will you feel once you have the debt out of your life? How will you feel once you have money saved for emergencies? How will you feel knowing you have control of your financial future?

8. Your budget will not always be perfect but it will keep you on track with knowing where your money is going. Advice to make this work: Don't give up! I'll say this again. Don't give up! There will be some struggles especially at the beginning but keep at it and you will start seeing the difference in how you connect with your money. After several years of budgeting, we still have times that it would be easier to just not budget but then we remember WHY we are doing this and it's so worth it!

☐

MORE TIPS FOR A SUCCESSFUL BUDGET

Doing a monthly budget can feel overwhelming. At times you might want to give up and just go back to spending without any idea where the money is going. As financial guru, Dave Ramsey said, "You've got to tell your money what to do or it will leave." How many times have you wondered where all the money has gone? Budgeting stops that guessing game! Here are some additional tips to create a successful budget.

1. Understand and know why you are budgeting. Do you want to pay off debt or save for emergencies? Knowing why you are budgeting will keep you motivated.

2. Have specific goals in mind. Set realistic goals with your money.

3. Find the right budgeting tools for you. There are several free options available online or Excel spreadsheets work great too.

4. Know your income. Include salary, commissions, items sold, etc.

5. Know your expenses. Include coffee stops, memberships, etc. Look back at your old bank statements to help gather the information.

6. Budget prior to spending. Don't spend and then develop your budget later. That leads to spending beyond your income.

7.   Review the budget often. You should review your budget a minimum of one to two times a month. Some months you may need to adjust your budget.

8.   Be patient. It took us 3 months to get the budget to work for us. Don't give up and keep working at it.

9.   Communication is important. Discuss and communicate about all expenses.

10.   Reach out for help. Consider working with a money coach or financial advisor if you are struggling to make the numbers work or need motivation to keep on top of your budget.

It's like trying to lose weight or quit smoking. With the right tools and mind set you can be successful with your budget!

SIMPLE WAYS TO FIND EXTRA MONEY FOR YOUR BUDGET

There are months that your budget can be really tight and it's a struggle to put extra money towards paying off debt or into your savings. Here is a simple way to find some extra money. Start digging through your unused STUFF and find things to sell! Yes, I call it "stuff" because we all have it around our homes.

You will be amazed how many things you can find in and around your home that you don't use or need anymore. It's costing you money by storing it so why wait. Start selling and turn it into extra dollars for your budget!

Check your closets... What about kids' clothes that are almost like new but don't fit anymore. Don't forget a dress or suit you only wore once but might look great on someone else. Have some vintage clothes from your high school years? I bet you can find a few pieces in your closet so start digging.

Toys... Do you still have toys laying around the house that your kids have outgrown? New parents are always looking for baby toys and activities that are gently used. If it still works and is in good condition people will be interested in buying it. Even if it doesn't work some buyers are looking for parts to replace on their own equipment.

Outdoor Equipment... Clean out the garage of unused bikes and sports equipment. Fill the tires and clean the equipment and you might be able to get a little more for it.

Electronics... New gaming systems, tablets and computers are great but don't hold on to your older version if it's just lying around collecting dust.

Antiques/Furniture... You might think that the old pottery bowl your Grandma used decades ago is not worth anything but it could be just what someone else is looking for to complete their set. Not using the recliner in the corner? It might look great in another person's house so why not sell it to them.

☐
WHERE TO SELL YOUR ITEMS?
There are several online options that you could try listing your items. Some include: Craigslist, Ebay or Facebook (many communities offer a Facebook garage sale page).

Offline try selling through your local paper; spread the word to your neighbors and coworkers; organize a yard sale.

This is a great way to make a little extra money to put in your savings or pay off debt. Bonus: You cleared your house of unused stuff that was cluttering your home!

☐

SIMPLE WAYS TO CUT MONTHLY ELECTRONIC COSTS

Below are three simple ways to cut cost on your monthly expenses so you can free up dollars in your budget.

Phones... Have you reviewed your cellphone or landline phone plan lately? Do you need all the extra features or the insurance? Carefully review your plans and see if there are areas that you can cut and save some money. It might even be time to check other providers and compare what they offer. If you have been with your provider for a long time, contact them and see if they have any deals or specials for you. My provider recently gave me a complimentary upgraded phone (no extra monthly fees) because I have been with them for over a decade. This saved me over $190.00!

Internet... So many devices in our home need the internet so it's important that it's reliable but it doesn't have to empty your wallet. There are many options available and with quite a variety of pricing and special deals for new accounts. It's good to know how much bandwidth you need. You might have a larger plan than you require. Visit websites or call local providers and find out what internet option is best for you and see if you can put a few extra dollars back in your wallet.

Television... Cable, satellite, streaming and good old fashion antennas can all provide us with great entertainment. You can really cut into your monthly budget here! Cable and satellite are typically more expensive than the other two options. If you really want to keep your cable or satellite check what is all included in your package. Maybe you can go to a lower package or see if they have any special deals. I contact our satellite provider about every 4-6 months to see what deals they have and I'm usually able to get a discount. Options like Netflix and Amazon Prime can be a less expensive option as is using an antenna.

Bundle Options... Some providers offer packages that cover phone, internet and television. Don't just assume they are a better deal as they may not meet your needs or could have a lot of extra fluff you won't even use but pay for it. We currently bundle our phone and internet which has saved us about $20 a month. They had additional packages that included satellite but that would have cost us double what we pay now. Compare the packages to buying the services individually and see what is best for you and saves you some money!!!

SOMETHING TO TRY!

Take a break from technology. Maybe it's time for a technology freeze. Turn off your cable or satellite for a month or switch to a lower data plan on your phone. Put the devices down and enjoy the book you have been meaning to read or engage in a deep conversation with a loved one. That's not only good for your budget but also for your soul.

FIVE SMALL CHANGES THAT WILL FREE UP CASH IN YOUR BUDGET

If you have recently started a monthly budget (hooray!) you will notice that some months, the money doesn't stretch as far as you need it too. Maybe you forgot about your Mom's birthday or the dog's annual physical. It would be easier to just grab the credit card and give up on the budget. I'm telling you, don't give in to the card!

As you get into a groove with your budget you will know how to plan ahead for these moments so they won't be as daunting. In the meantime, I'm going to share with you five small changes you can make in your monthly or even weekly routine to help you find some extra dollars. So, put down that plastic card and get ready to take back some dollars for your budget.

1.   Car wash…Having a clean shiny vehicle is great but going to the car wash can add up if you get the deluxe package. When your budget is tight, get out your sponge and bucket and wash the vehicle at home.   This can also be a fun family activity. Who doesn't enjoy a water fight on a hot summer day!

2.   Lunches…Going out to lunch might sound better then leftovers, but if you eat out several times a week the money can fly out of your wallet quite quickly. Start packing a lunch every day or limit your eating out to just one day a week and you will definitely free up some cash. Think about how much healthier you can make your lunches by preparing them yourself.

3. Hair salon…Who doesn't love to get pampered! It can be quite expensive to keep up with your hair care needs and all the other beauty regimens. Instead of getting your hair cut every four weeks try to extend it to every six weeks. You can save a huge amount of money coloring your hair at home and limiting the salon visits to a couple times a year. Many boxed hair color kits are a professional grade color (there are some great inexpensive options on Amazon) and cost less than $10.00. Do the math and see how much you can save by just making this change.

4. Beverages…If Starbucks or gas station beverages are part of your morning ritual it might be time to change things up when your budget is tight. I love my morning coffee and tea but we all know the cost can add up quickly if you are a frequent coffee buyer. Cut back to once a week or even less and start making your own coffee or tea before you leave home. If you stop for a large soda every week, consider going to the grocery store and buy a case vs. individual servings. This is typically cheaper and now you can easily grab one on your way out the door.

5. Date Night…I strongly believe in date nights! Having the one-on-one time with your spouse, fiancé, a great friend or other family members is a great chance to catch up on your lives and strengthen your bond.

If your budget is tight there are many great options that don't have to cost a lot of money for an awesome date night. Instead of going out to eat at a pricey restaurant why not enjoy some tasty eats at a local burger joint or grab some subs and have a picnic. If your date night usually includes some dancing or concerts, check the local entertainment guide for free community activities or dances. You can even throw a great dance party at home. Bonus: You get to pick the music and you don't have to worry about people seeing your crazy dance moves!

Try to focus your date night on building your connection with the person you are with and not about the places you go.

TEN HACKS TO STRETCH YOUR DOLLAR

I'm going to share with you some great tips that can stretch your dollar a little further with these hacks around your home.

1.   When making meals, use more items like vegetables, pasta, and rice and fewer items like meat and seafood which typically are more expensive. Can't think of any ideas? There are some great recipes on Pinterest, Yummly and other online recipe sites. Some of our favorites are noodles with a homemade marinara or cream sauce or a colorful vegetable stir fry. So good!

2.   Turn the thermostat down when you leave the house for long periods of time and during the night. Get cold easily? Throw on an extra layer of clothes or blankets. During the summer months avoid cranking up the air conditioner. Closing the blinds and curtains during the day can help keep it cool inside.

3.   Cut items in half for double the use. Paper towels, dryer sheets and baby wipes are great examples. Some of the paper towel sheets are really big so cutting them in half still leaves a nice size towel to clean up spills.

4.   Do a babysitting swap with trusted friends or neighbors. Quality babysitters can really cost you a lot of money. By swapping services with trusted friends and neighbors you can save on that cost. It's also a great way for the neighborhood kids to build some great friendships.

5.   Eat the food in your freezer and pantry. Don't forget about that pork roast and frozen vegetables you purchased last month that is sitting in the back of the freezer. Your pantry might have great side dishes to go with it. Check your supplies on hand before heading out for dinner.

6.   Plant a vegetable garden. Fresh from your garden vegetables are such a treat. Seeds and starter plants can be fairly inexpensive and you don't need a green thumb to grow your own harvest. This alone can make a big impact on your grocery bill.

7.   Make homemade house cleaners and laundry soap. There are an abundant number of recipes online for homemade house cleaners and laundry soap. Using natural cleaners like vinegar is not only less expensive but healthier for you too.

8.   Reuse & re-purpose paper and magazines. Paper with printing on one side is great for jotting down notes vs. buying designer pads. Use newspapers or magazines to protect packed items instead of buying the spendy bubble wrap.

9.   Prepare freezer meals so you are less tempted to order out when you don't feel like cooking. We all have nights where cooking is the last thing we want to do. By planning ahead, you can pull out a prepared freezer meal and let the oven do the work. You just saved a good chunk of money by not eating out and you don't have to leave your house so that saves you money on transportation as well!

10. Keep things organized. A little organization keeps extra dollars in your pocket. Knowing where you have things placed will keep you from going out and purchasing something you already own. How many times have you purchased something because you just couldn't find it? Or maybe you forgot you already owned it because it wasn't where it belongs.

When you budget monthly you will see the impact every dollar has towards achieving your financial goals!

AVOID THE WINTER MONEY BLUES

For many people winter months can be a struggle because of rising utility bills. In addition, credit card spending often increases due to holiday shopping and entertaining. With some advance planning you don't have to let those bills bring on the winter money blues. I have some great ideas to help you feel warm and fuzzy this winter and prevent those extra dreaded payments.

Plan ahead... Since you know Christmas and cooler temps are coming, start saving money in advance. A great way to do this is to take a set amount out of your paycheck each month and apply it towards those costs. For example, each month take out $50-$75 and put it in a savings account or envelope marked for holiday shopping and/or utility bills. If you do this for the entire year you would have up to $900 saved! That's a big chunk of money for holiday gift giving and utility bills. Start this savings plan today!

Spend less... It's great to be a giver but try and find ways to cut back on your spending during the holidays. With my family we draw names so we have less gifts to purchase. We also do small stocking stuffers for nieces and nephews vs. buying more expensive items. Consider making homemade crafts or offer a service like babysitting your brother's kids or cooking a meal for your neighbor. Use your special talents as part of your gift giving. If you plan to purchase gifts, then watch for sales and consider checking out sites like Groupon or Ebates to save more money.

Reduce Utilities.... Being warm and cozy in your home feels great but not when you have a hefty gas and electric bill. That can leave you feeling cold! Consider keeping your house a little cooler and put on an extra layer of clothes. Get out those warm fuzzy socks you got for Christmas last year. Unplug items that you are not using (extra lamps, chargers, etc...) and remember to turn off the lights when you leave a room.

Budget.... If your holiday spending and utilities are still eating up a lot of your money then it's time to find other areas to reduce your spending in your budget. Instead of going out for that holiday dinner with your friends, consider having a potluck or cookie exchange. There is a plethora of entertaining options during the holidays like live performances and new movies. Instead of getting out the credit card for the higher priced activities, consider renting a couple holiday movies from the library and have a little festive party at home. This saves money on the tickets, the extravagant dinner and a new outfit you probably would want to purchase for your night out.

Increase Your Income... If each year you struggle with paying bills around and after the holidays, then consider increasing your income. Many retail stores are looking for holiday help or see if you can get in some overtime hours at your job. If you don't want to leave your home during the cold temps there are online opportunities as well. Why not consider babysitting or dog sitting at your house. You may have a talent that could make you some extra income so why not give it a try!

WHAT IF WE STILL CAN'T PAY OUR BILLS?

When you can't pay your bills, you feel worried, stressed and maybe even embarrassed. This pressure can lead us to make poor decisions with our money. This does not define who you are as a person. You can pull out of this and get it under control. Believe in yourself and in your partner.

When your expenses are more than your income it is not time to give up on making your budget work. All your doing is ignoring the problem. It will continue to fester and get out of control if you don't deal with it now.

This book contains many tips for cutting your monthly costs but sometimes it still might not be enough. The next step is to sit down with your spouse and determine a plan.

Discuss together which bills are a priority. Those should include house, electricity, water, basic food supplies. Do you have enough income to cover those costs?

Next, talk about which bills you could hold off on paying or pay a smaller amount for that month. Contact the bill companies and let them know that you are serious about taking care of this bill but you are unable to make a payment or a full payment this month.

Do your best to not allow your emotions to take over during this time. You will get through this but it takes work and determination.

TEACHING KIDS ABOUT MONEY

Young kids are like sponges and are capable of learning and remembering important life skills. With guidance they learn how to tie their shoes, ride a bike and even solve algebra problems. Some of these skills are easy and almost come naturally while others take months and even years of practice and determination to master. One skill we often forget to teach our kids is how to be smart with their money.

In the past, my husband and I have made many not-so-smart decisions when it comes to money. Now that we have taken the steps to be on track with our finances we want to help our kids avoid some of those same money mistakes. Here are a few ways that we are teaching them this important life skill.

Budget…Every month we prepare our budget. My husband and I will go through every detail together to determine the right budget for us. Not only do the kids see us meeting but we also ask their input on items that affect them. For example, if we want to plan a family adventure we may decide together how much we will spend and what we might have to adjust that month to not go over budget.

Spend, Save & Give Accounts: The kids each have three accounts that they determine how much money they want to put into each one. These are dollars they receive as gifts or for doing extra chores at home.

Spend... This is their play money. They can use it to buy new toys, electronic gadgets or whatever their heart desires. Our son had a goal to buy a go-kart. He was ecstatic the day he had enough to pay for his half of the go-kart. My husband and I thought this new ride sounded fun so we agreed to pay for half of it so we could sneak in a few rides too!

It took a lot of discipline for him to not spend that money every time we walked the isles of Target. A few times he almost gave in but then remembered how much he wanted that go-kart and he would put the toy back on the shelf. As adults we even struggle with that!

FYI... The items he put back on the shelf ended up being great ideas for birthday and Christmas presents.

Save... With this account the kids are saving up for their first car and extra cash towards college. The kids tend to put the most in this fund unless they are saving up for something fun like a go-kart. They are also earning interest on this money so they are excited to know it's growing. We have a few more years before our kids will be driving (thank goodness!!!) and going off to college but they know cars and college are expensive so they are glad to have a head start.

Give... Our kids love this account! This money is for them to donate to something or someone else that needs the money. It warms my heart seeing my kids freely handing over money to their church or for a school fundraiser. In the past we would often give them the money to donate. I now believe they have more of a connection with that kind and generous act if they are using their own money and determining who receives it and how much to give.

Just like riding their bikes, kids are going to take risks and occasionally trip up with their money as they get older. Our goal is to help guide them so they know how to get back on track and keep cruising along the journey of life.

MONEY FIGHTS
How to Avoid Them

Money is one of the leading causes of fights in a marriage. Unfortunately, many of those arguments lead to separation or divorce between couples.

Nobody wants to fight with their loved ones about money but sometimes our emotions take over and we find ourselves putting on the boxing gloves. Before we started budgeting, we often had arguments over money. It was very draining on all of us. Kids pick up on those things. I don't know about you, but that is not the example we want to set for our kids. Since we enhanced our communication as a couple and learned to stay on track with our budget, our arguments are so minimal. Honestly, I can't remember the last time we argued.

I'm going to share with you a few great tips that my husband and I use to keep our cool and avoid a potential boxing match. Pull off the gloves and use these tips to avoid the money fights.

Let's say your spouse or fiancé just made a financial decision that has you steaming. Maybe they just purchased a large flat screen TV when you have been working towards paying off your student loans. Or maybe they just informed you they borrowed $1,000 to their cousin who is not working right now and you will probably never see that money again. You get the picture! There are many scenarios that can leave us irritated and wanting to yell at them for their decision.

I'm going to give you a very important tip... Don't attack them on the spot even though you want to bring out the claws. There is a right time and place to talk about it. Many money fights could be avoided by choosing wisely when and where to discuss your financial situation.

10-minute rule... Have you heard of the cooling down period? Take 10 minutes or more to clear your mind and calm yourself before talking to them about it.

Think before you speak... You know the term "don't put your foot in your mouth" right? It applies here. Think about your response before you speak. Avoid words that sound like you are attacking them or treating them like a young child who needs a time out.

Express your feelings... It's important to think before you speak but it's also important to express how you feel. During the cooling down period think about why his/her action has you so upset. Is it because they made a decision without you? Is it because you were really hoping to have your loans paid off in the next couple months? You need to ask yourself these questions and express those concerns with your spouse. This will help them to understand your frustrations.

Pick a calming location to talk... Find a neutral location to talk. Don't stand next to the big screen TV that has already made you angry. Find a place that both of you will feel a little more relaxed. Maybe it's a favorite coffee shop, on the patio or on the couch. A calming environment will help you keep your cool as you talk.

Remember we are not perfect and our spouse is not either so we need to work together and keep moving forward through these hiccups and trudge on with your financial goals.

CONNECT AS A COUPLE TO WIN WITH YOUR MONEY

No Keeping Secrets About Debt
Be open and honest with your partner about your debt. They will eventually find out so don't put this tension on your relationship. If you are engaged don't wait until the wedding day. Start talking about your finances NOW.

Spender vs. Saver
Talk about your spending habits together. It's important to know if your partner is a spender or a saver. Does taking out a loan feel like no big deal or does it scare you to owe money to someone else? Many relationships have a spender & saver so take time to discuss it now. You may have to compromise in some financial decisions. FYI...There is no room for judgement in a marriage!

Communicate Your Feelings
If you are not happy with a financial decision your partner made without you then talk with them about it. Be smart about when you decide to have this conversation. You don't want them to feel like they are under attack. Don't wait too long either as it can fester and turn into an unnecessary argument. Being open and honest with each other is very important in a marriage.

"You + Me = We"
When you both made the decision to become united in marriage you decided to become a team (aka: WE). All big financial decisions should be made together.

You can still allocate a monthly personal fund that you alone get to spend. This personal fund is for each of you to buy something "guilt free". But all other expenses/saving decisions should be done as a team.

Forgiveness

We have all made some not so smart decisions. Learn to forgive yourself and your spouse for past mistakes. Bringing up bad financial decisions made five years ago isn't good for anyone and especially your marriage. Move forward together and don't let the past overtake your future.

Budget Planning Dates

A budget is a very important tool in taking control of your money. With a budget you will be able to pay off debt faster and save for your dreams. The budget needs to be a team effort so plan budgeting date nights every month. Find a place you enjoy like a café, park or even your living room. The key to making a budget work is to remember that You + Me = We!

Starting a budget together can be overwhelming! I know this from our own experience. Communication as a couple is the key to making it work in order to see the progress you want for your financial future!

☐

FOCUS ON YOUR LIFE AND NOT THEIRS

All around us we are watching other people build new homes, drive expensive vehicles take their family on dream vacations. Years ago, you could close the door and hide behind the blinds, but now it's all around us. With technology and social media, we continuously get to see and hear about what others have that you don't. I used to be jealous of their lives. I felt it wasn't fair and I deserved everything they have.

That has changed! I no longer want someone else's life. I have chosen to focus on my life; my story. It can mentally and financially destroy you focusing on what others have that you don't. Do you really know their full story? Is it all for show? Many of your friends and family could be putting up a good front while they are struggling personally and financially. We tend to show off our best moments for others to see.

Put your focus and energy in building your story; your legacy. Learn to be content and thankful for the people and things you have in your life. This transformation allows you to take control of your future and writing your own life story.

It's time for you to take control of your financial future! Budgeting is one of the key steps to get you there. You are now equipped with some great tools and tips to help you rock your budget.

YOU HAVE THE POWER WITHIN TO CHANGE YOUR FINANCIAL FUTURE!

DEBT WORKSHEET

NAME OF DEBT	TOTAL DUE	INTEREST RATE	PAYMENT DUE

DISCUSSION QUESTIONS FOR COUPLES

Do we want to pay off our debt early?

How would we feel if we didn't have these extra bills each month?

Are we ready to keep additional debt out of our life?

What would we do with the extra money each month if we didn't have these payments?

ADDITIONAL RESOURCES TO STAY ON TRACK

BUDGET & MONEY COMMUNICATION HELP: If you need additional assistance with making your budget work or you are struggling as a couple to get on track with your money contact a money coach at **www.roseannbaisley.com**.

RETIREMENT & INVESTMENT HELP: It's important to look to the future and your retirement. Don't assume you're going to be okay financially. No matter what your age, you need to plan for your retirement. Consider reaching out to a financial advisor that will work with you to meet your goals.

TAX HELP: Are you receiving a large tax return? It might seem great at the time but think about all the extra money you have been paying in all year long. That money could have been applied towards your debt or put into a savings account. Contact an accountant that will help you determine what is best for your financial situation.

INSURANCE HELP: It's important to make sure you have the right coverage for insurance. Do you currently have life insurance or disability insurance? Do you have enough coverage on your home? Contact your insurance agent to review your policies.

If you would like to know who we use for these services (Love our reps! No, they didn't pay me to say that.) send me a message and I can get you their names. Contact me at coach@roseannbaisley.com.

☐

ABOUT THE AUTHOR

Roseann Baisley is a certified life coach and transformation coach through Universal Coach Institute. Roseann has used her personal experience to successfully guide others in taking control of their finances. She offers one on one coaching with individuals and couples who want to be proactive vs. reactive with their money. She lives in Cold Spring with her amazing husband, two awesome kids and their energetic dog.

CONTACT INFORMATION

Roseann Baisley, CLC
Roseann Baisley Coaching & Consulting
coach@roseannbaisley.com
www.roseannbaisley.com

www.ingramcontent.com/pod-product-compliance
Lightning Source LLC
Chambersburg PA
CBHW070420190526
45169CB00003B/1343